D1808298

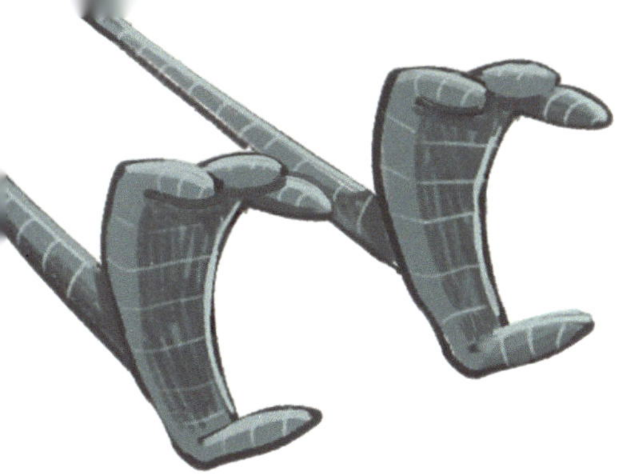

A Right Royal 'Roach Trip !

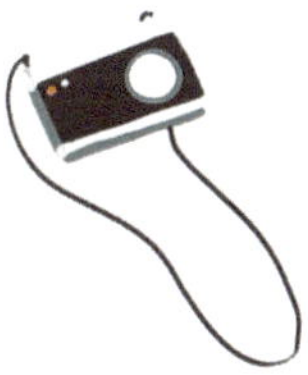

SUSIE VIOLET

illustration by Alex Patrick

Published by
Twinky & Hoobie Publishing

Copyright 2020 by Susie Violet
Published by Twinky & Hoobie Publishing
ISBN: 978-1-9993232-8-8

Illustrations by Alex Patrick

All rights reserved
No part of this book may be reproduced in any form or by any electronic or mechanical means,
including information storage and retrieval systems, without permission in writing from the author.
The only exception is by a reviewer, who may quote short excerpts in a review.

Creative and Print by SpiffingCovers Ltd.

"If you think you are too little to make a big difference, try sleeping with a mosquito in the room."

Pedro the little cockroach,
Was feeling chirpy and chipper,
He looked at all the bright lights,
Through a haze that twinkled like glitter.

'We are BOLD travellers,' Pedro said,
'On a mission to discover.'
Enrico turned to his best friend.
Then they looked around in wonder.

'Arrrrrrrrrriba,' Pedro whooped.
'Let's go and explore.'
Pedro's pal Enrico yelled,
'Look, a riverboat! Quick, jump aboard.'

THAMES CRUISE

The 'roaches crept across the deck,
To where a creature sat.
Pedro smiled, and the pear-shaped figure said
'Hiya, I'm RUBY RAT.'

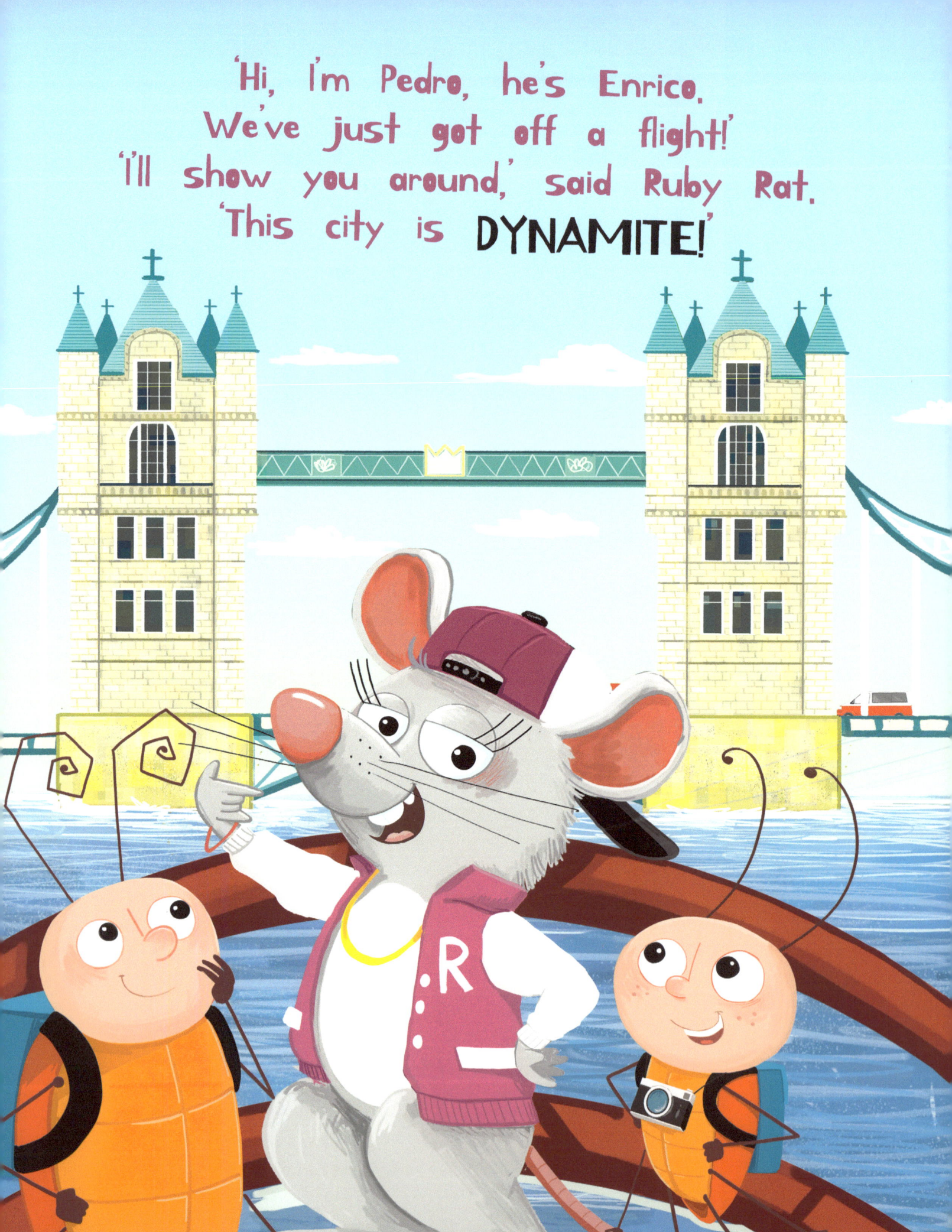

'Hi, I'm Pedro, he's Enrico.
We've just got off a flight!'
'I'll show you around,' said Ruby Rat.
'This city is DYNAMITE!'

The boat *whipped* up the RIVER THAMES,
Their excitement grew stronger.
THE LONDON EYE and TOWER BRIDGE,
Were reflected in the water.

They arrived at THE TOWER OF LONDON,
And stared with awe and surprise.

Suddenly, a raven SWOOPED in,
And took them up towards the skies.

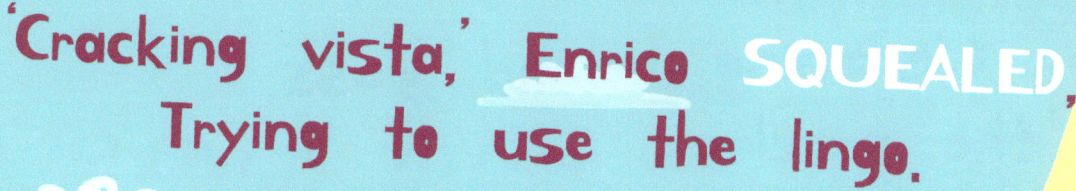

'Cracking vista,' Enrico SQUEALED,
Trying to use the lingo.

They took in the views, truly amused,
Before being DROPPED through
a stone window.

Glistening behind glass,
Sat the priceless CROWN JEWELS,
With over 140 gems to see,
All the little bugs could say was:

'Cooooooool!'

All of a sudden, a BEEFEATER shouted,
'Stop that robber!' as a man ran by.
Pedro cried, 'Follow my lead!'
'Ruby, trip up the bad guy.'

The bugs LEAPED up high,
With a funny little dance.
They flapped their wings with fat big grins.
He did not stand a chance.

They buzzed around
the bandit's head,
And landed on his nose.

Ruby Rat ran
between his legs;
He fell FLAT on his
back and then froze.

'We've got him, thank you nibblers!'
The Beefeater blurted.
You have really saved the day,
And the Bobbies have been alerted.

To BUCKINGHAM PALACE,
The heroes were escorted.
In the Gold State Coach,
Drawn by **eight royal horses**.

The palace was full of joy. THE QUEEN was delighted. 'To award you with the highest thanks, You are all to be **KNIGHTED.**'

The three little chums stooped before the Queen,
And knelt for a tiny sword,

A sight NO ONE had ever seen.
As they bowed, the big crowd ROARED.

Rise, Sir Pedro; rise Sir Enrico,
And, of course, Dame Ruby.
I speak on behalf of England,
For you have done your duty.

The Queen happily announced,
'You must all stay for tea.
I royally do insist,' said the Queen,
'... the cakes are **SO SCRUMMY**.'

The excitement was all too much;
Ruby almost fainted.
'It would be an honour,' Pedro BEAMED.
Enrico felt elated.

Ruby peeled herself from the floor,
And SCOFFED at an incredible pace.
The state banquet was full of treats,
BUT their table manners were A DISGRACE.

After tea they had to dash,
So much to do and see.
'I'll show you around on a LONDON BUS,'
Dame Ruby said, 'Come with me.'

A final tour of this great city,
And a stroll through Hyde Park.
It had been a ROLLER-COASTER adventure.
Seeing nearly EVERY single landmark.

It was now time for the three amigos,
to finally say goodbye.
Ruby dropped them off at The Ritz,
And left with a tear in her eye.

The little bugs had earned a rest.
What an AMAZING day!
It was all beyond their WILDEST dreams.
But it was time to hit the hay.

Pedro nuzzled into a blanket,
Enrico blocked out the light.
Tomorrow would be ANOTHER adventure,
But for now, they said 'night-night.'

THE END

`Roach

LONDON NEWS

COCKROACH HEROS

HEROS

Trip!

Thank you!

As always, thank you to my husband Robbie, and children Elsie & Henry for their zany ideas and support, especially when we are on our Roach trip adventures.

An enormous debt of gratitude goes to the creative genius James Wlllis. Thank you for being truly amazing on every level.

Thank you to my Mum & Dad for giving me the drive and tenacity to keep pushing through every hurdle.

And finally, another huge thank you to Victoria Lee, my editor, whose input has been invaluable to this process.

Lightning Source UK Ltd.
Milton Keynes UK
UKHW050512090822
407032UK00002B/39

* 9 7 8 1 9 9 9 3 2 3 2 8 8 *